First Aladdin Paperbacks edition January 2003

Copyright © 1999 by Faith Ringgold

ALADDIN PAPERBACKS
An imprint of Simon & Schuster
Children's Publishing Division
1230 Avenue of the Americas
New York, NY 10020

Also available in a Simon & Schuster Books for Young Readers hardcover edition.
The text of this book was set in 14-point Bembo semibold.
The illustrations were rendered in acrylics on canvas paper.

Manufactured in the United States of America
8 10 9 7

The Library of Congress has cataloged the hardcover edition as follows:
Ringgold, Faith.
If a bus could talk ; the story of Rosa Parks / written and illustrated by Faith Ringgold.—1st ed.
p. cm.
Summary: A biography of the African American woman and civil rights worker whose refusal to
give up her seat on a bus led to a boycott which lasted more than a year in Montgomery, Alabama.
ISBN 0-689-81892-0 (hc)
1. Parks, Rosa, 1913—Juvenile literature. 2. Afro-Americans—Alabama—Montgomery—
Biography—Juvenile literature. 3. Civil rights workers—Alabama—Montgomery—Biography—
Juvenile literature. 4. Afro-Americans—Civil rights—Alabama—Montgomery—Juvenile
literature. 5. Segregation in transportation—Alabama—Montgomery—History—20th century—
Juvenile literature. 6. Montgomery (Ala.)—Race relations—Juvenile literature 7. Montgomery
(Ala.)—Biography—Juvenile literature. [1. Parks, Rosa, 1913–. 2. Afro-Americans—Biography.
3. Civil rights workers. 4. Segregation in transportation. 5. Montgomery (Ala.)—Race relations.
6. Women—Biography.] I. Title.
F334.M753R56 1999
323'.092—dc21
[b]
98-22578
ISBN 0-689-85676-8 (Aladdin pbk.)

This story is dedicated to Rosa Parks and all of the known and unknown men, women, and children of the Civil Rights movement who, through their singular acts of courage, made it possible for black people to vote; take a seat on a bus, in a movie theater, or at a lunch counter; and get a hotel room, just like any other American citizen.

*T*his morning a strange-looking bus pulled up at my stop. It didn't look anything like my usual bus, but it was on time and I didn't want to be late for school, so I decided to take it. The door opened and a voice called out, "Step on up, young lady." I got on thinking, *I'll ask the driver which bus this is.*

BUS STOP

But the driver was not in his seat. I paid my fare and looked around for him. There were lots of passengers, but their faces weren't familiar. I started to ask one of them if I was on the right bus, but before I could, the door closed and the bus pulled away from the curb—with no one in the driver's seat! The sudden start sent me reeling down the aisle and I landed in a seat, holding on for dear life. None of the other passengers seemed to notice anything was wrong. "Stop this bus and let me off!" I shouted. "I want a bus with a driver!"

"Please don't take that seat, Marcie," someone said.

"How do you know my name? Which one of you is speaking?" I asked, looking around.

But the passengers were talking among themselves, reading, or just staring out the window.

"This is a special bus, Marcie, and you are sitting in a special seat reserved for a very special person."

"Amen! Amen!" chorused the passengers.

"What bus is this?" I asked.

"This used to be the Cleveland Avenue bus, but now it's the Rosa Parks bus. She is the patron saint of the Civil Rights movement. One day a year we reserve that seat in her name. Take another seat and I will tell you all about her."

Now the voice seemed to be coming from the bus itself. I could hardly believe it—I was on a talking bus! Trembling with fear but curious as I could be, I took a seat across the aisle and settled down to hear this remarkable story. . . .

"Rosa McCauley, the first child of James and Leona McCauley, was born on February 4, 1913, in Tuskeegee, Alabama. When Rosa was two years old her father, a skilled carpenter and house builder, left the family and went up North looking for work. Her mother took Rosa and Sylvester, her baby brother, to live on their grandfather's small farm in Pine Level, Alabama. They worked hard there, raising chickens, calves, vegetables, nuts, and fruit. Rosa helped her grandfather clear weeds and tend the crops. The family also picked cotton in neighboring fields.

"From Rosa's earliest childhood she could remember scary nights when the Ku Klux Klan, a band of hateful white men dressed in white hooded robes, would ride past their farm shooting off rifles to frighten the black people. Rosa knew that the Klan had burned churches and beaten, tortured, and lynched many black people. There were times when Rosa's family slept in their clothes so they could run if the Klan decided to burn their house down in the middle of the night.

"Despite these fearful conditions, Rosa's grandfather was an outspoken old man who made it known that he had a loaded shotgun and was not afraid to use it to defend his home and family. Grandfather Sylvester instilled a sense of pride in his children and grandchildren, and in Rosa most of all. Rosa was a nice little girl who loved praise, but she hated the disrespectful way whites often treated black people. One day a white boy threatened to punch her, and Rosa picked up a rock and threatened to hit him back if he did. When her grandmother heard about this she was very afraid, because she knew something like that might cause Rosa to be lynched one day.

"When Rosa was six years old, she went to school. Her school had fifty to sixty children in one room and only one teacher. In Pine Level, Alabama, school for black children only went up to the sixth grade, and it was open only five months out of the year, while school for white children went through the twelfth grade and was open for nine months. And the white children could take a bus to school while the black children often had to walk a long way. However, Rosa's mother, Leona, had plans for Rosa's education. Leona was a teacher in a one-room school in the village of Spring Hill. To teach there she had to travel a long distance and then be away from her children all week. But she saved up so Rosa could further her education.

"When Rosa was eleven, she went to Miss White's School for Girls in Montgomery, Alabama. Several years later Rosa went on to high school at Alabama State Teacher's College for Negroes. She had to drop out of school when first her grandmother and then her mother became ill. Rosa's mother got well but her grandmother later died.

"After Leona recovered, Rosa went back to school and got her high school diploma, but it would be a few years before Rosa could find a job using her typing and writing skills. So she took in sewing and did alterations at the Montgomery Fair department store.

"One day on the way home from work the bus driver told Rosa to get off and enter at the back of the bus after she had paid her fare. Then he drove off, leaving her in the street. This was common practice then. It is no wonder that black people would often walk a mile or more to and from work rather than ride the segregated buses.

"The buses were the worst form of segregation because black people could only sit in the back of the bus. If there were no whites in the middle section blacks could sit there, but only if no white people were left standing. Black people couldn't sit in the same row with whites, even if there was an empty seat in that row.

"It was during those times I got to know and love Rosa Parks," said the talking bus. "She was a great lady with quiet dignity despite all the cruelty she faced because of the color of her skin.

"But then something good happened—Rosa married a very nice man named Raymond Parks. Parks, as she called him, was a black man like Grandfather Sylvester—he demanded to be treated with respect. Parks was light-skinned and had grown up in an all-white neighborhood. Although he looked like a white person, he was not allowed to go to the white school, and the nearest black school was too far away. So he had been taught to read and write by his mother. Despite the fact that he had very little formal education, Parks was well spoken and well read on the important issues affecting his people. It was Parks who encouraged Rosa to return to school and graduate.

"Raymond Parks, a barber by trade, had been a longtime member of the NAACP, the National Association for the Advancement of Colored People. Mrs. Parks soon became a member too. In no time she was appointed secretary of the Montgomery branch and could use her education to help her people. She also served as youth leader and organized a city-wide youth conference.

"Parks worked hard to free four young men called the Scottsboro Boys, who were jailed for a crime they did not commit. Parks was also an activist for voter registration and he and Rosa held regular meetings of the Voter's League in their home. That was how Rosa finally registered to vote after being turned down three times before.

"One fateful day (December 1, 1955), Mrs. Parks took this very bus home from work. The bus driver, whose name was James Blake, told Mrs. Parks to get up and give her seat to a white man. There were other black people sitting in the same section and all of them would have to get up so that the white man could sit down. Rosa knew that the segregation laws were unfair and, right then and there, she decided to do something about it. She told the driver she would not give up her seat. This was the same bus driver who had wronged her before.

"When Mrs. Parks refused to give up her seat, Blake called the police and had her arrested and taken to jail for breaking the segregation laws.

"It is for this singular act of courage that, one day a year, Mrs. Parks's seat has been reserved," said the talking bus. "And why we don't want to see Blake driving this bus ever again."

"Amen! Amen!" chorused the passengers.

"How long did Mrs. Parks have to stay in jail?" I asked.

"Not long, Marcie. When Mr. E. D. Nixon, the head of the Montgomery branch of the NAACP, heard of Mrs. Parks's arrest, he paid her bail and she was released. He asked her to help with a boycott to change the segregation laws. Rosa was happy to be a part of a city-wide effort to end segregated buses. Mr. E. D. Nixon also asked the Women's Political Council and the town's black ministers to help organize and promote what came to be known the world over as the Montgomery Bus Boycott.

"One of the ministers was the pastor at the Dexter Avenue Baptist Church, a young man named Dr. Martin Luther King, Jr. Mr. E. D. Nixon asked him to lead the boycott because he was new to the town and had great promise. The Dexter Avenue Baptist Church drew a large crowd the night Dr. King told the people about the boycott. This was the beginning of Dr. King's leadership in the Civil Rights movement and the beginning of his many memorable speeches.

"On this day Dr. King said, 'We are tired of being segregated and humiliated, tired of being kicked about by the brutal feet of oppression.'

"For 381 days—more than a year—black people in Montgomery either walked or arranged their own car pools instead of taking the buses. Without the black passengers the buses were almost empty, and the city lost a lot of money. The Montgomery Bus Boycott was working!"

"Amen! Amen!" said the passengers. "We know, we were there."

"But as a result of the boycott Dr. Martin Luther King, Jr. was arrested and his home was bombed. Many others were arrested, too, and threatened with hateful letters, phone calls, and bombings.

The Montgomery Bus Boycott was the beginning of a national movement in which people of every race organized protests against segregation in their own towns. The boycotts spread to department stores where black people were not allowed to return articles of clothing they had bought, or to try on clothes before buying them."

"You mean Miss Rosa could not try on a pair of shoes or return a dress that did not fit?" I asked.

"Yes, Marcie. I know it's difficult for young people today to understand what life under the segregation laws was really like. There were 'eat-ins' too, where black people and white sympathizers would sit at 'For Whites Only' lunch counters and have food poured over their heads by the hissing crowds.

"But there was no sadder sight on a hot summer day than black children outside a public swimming pool displaying a 'For Whites Only' sign.

"Mrs. Parks's case finally reached the highest court in our land, and on November 13, 1956, the U.S. Supreme Court ruled that segregation on public buses was against the law. A little more than a month later the boycott ended. Black people no longer had to ride in the back of the bus, but the struggle for equal rights was not over. Rosa lost her twenty-five-dollar-a-week job at the Montgomery Fair department store, and she continued to receive threatening phone calls and letters.

"A year later Rosa and Raymond Parks moved to Detroit, where Rosa worked for Congressman John Conyers of Michigan. There she was able to help homeless people find decent housing, jobs, and community services.

"Mrs. Parks's struggle for equal rights continued. On August 28, 1963, at Dr. King's March on Washington, Rosa Parks was honored with a 'Tribute to Women' award by A. Philip Randolph. However, she was not asked to speak.

"And later, when she heard on the radio that Dr. King had been shot, Rosa wept in her mother's arms.

"Many tributes and awards have been given to this gentle, courageous woman. A bronze bust of Mrs. Parks is installed at the Smithsonian Institution in Washington, D.C. She was awarded the Spingarn Medal, the Martin Luther King, Jr. Nonviolent Peace Prize, the Eleanor Roosevelt Woman of Courage Award, and the Presidential Medal of Freedom. Mrs. Parks has received countless honorary degrees, plaques, and honors for her valiant act of courage and unceasing dedication to freedom. But what this old bus is proudest of is that Cleveland Avenue, the street this bus ran on, has been renamed Rosa Parks Boulevard.

"In addition to all this, once a year we get together to celebrate the great lady's birthday."

"Amen! Amen!" said the passengers. "We know, we were there."

And just like that, the bus stopped and Mrs. Parks herself got on! All the passengers stood up to meet her. And when she greeted them by name—Parks, E. D. Nixon, Dr. King, and the rest—I remembered them from her story. The once unfamiliar passengers now had faces I would never forget.

"I am so excited to meet you, Mrs. Parks," I said gleefully. "You really are the mother of the Civil Rights movement, and I am so lucky to be here. May I ask what gave you such a strong belief in freedom?"

"My belief in freedom goes way back to the days when my mother used to sing the old Negro spiritual, 'O Freedom Over Me,'" said Mrs. Parks. "Let's sing it together."

O freedom

O freedom

O freedom

O freedom over me

And before I'd be a slave

I'd be buried in my grave

And go home to my Lord

and be free.

"Now it's time for you to cut your birthday cake, Mrs. Parks," said the talking bus. Mrs. Parks closed her eyes, drew a deep breath, and blew out all the candles.

"Happy Birthday, Mrs. Parks," said the passengers, "and may our dreams of freedom and equal opportunity for all people come true. We love you and we thank you for being the lady who, by sitting down, inspired people all over the world to stand up for freedom. Amen! Amen! We know, we were there."

By the time the talking bus reached my school, my head was crammed full of all the things that had happened. When I got up this morning, little did I know that I would be attending Mrs. Parks's birthday party on the very bus she was arrested on. I can't wait to tell my class about this!